Mrs Wordsmith ®

THE **BOOK** OF **BIG** FEELINGS

Bearnice

Bogart

Brick

Plato

Yin & Yang

Grit

Stax

Armie

Oz

MEET THE
CHARACTERS

Scan to find out more!

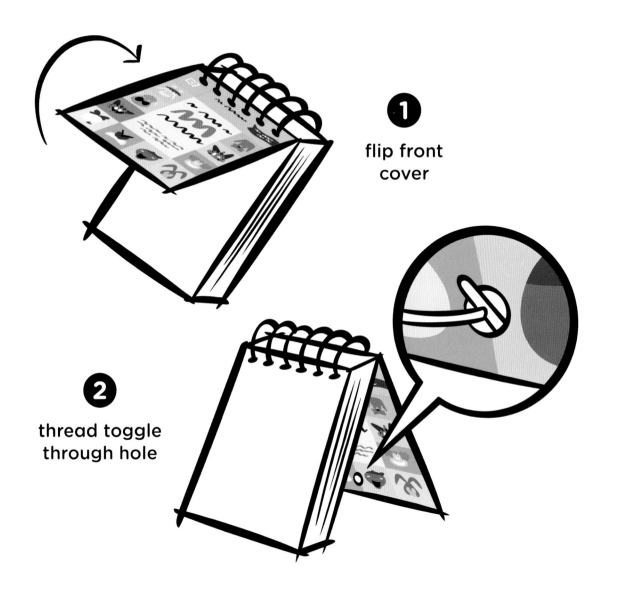

1

flip front
cover

2

thread toggle
through hole

Now, place the book on a surface
and discover a new word every day.

GET STARTED!

WHAT IS SOCIAL AND EMOTIONAL LEARNING?

Childhood is a time of rapid biological, social, cognitive and emotional change. Social and emotional learning (SEL) is critical to making sure that kids thrive in the classroom, in the playground and at home – preparing them for life in the ever-changing terrain of the modern world.

SEL is an integral part of education and human development. It is the process through which all young people acquire and apply the knowledge, skills and attitudes to develop healthy identities, manage emotions, feel and show empathy for others, establish and maintain supportive relationships and make responsible decisions. All these skills help children become more self-aware, exercise self-control and develop interpersonal skills that are vital for school, work and life-long success.

People with strong social and emotional skills are better able to cope with everyday challenges, from effective problem-solving to greater self-discipline, as well as greater emotion management skills.

Search "CASEL" online to find out more about social and emotional learning and the five core competencies identified by researchers at the Collaborative for Academic, Social and Emotional Learning.

THE MAGIC OF WORDS

This is a book full of words and full of feeling. At Mrs Wordsmith, we know that kids who can talk about their emotions confidently and accurately grow into well-rounded, flourishing young people.

Learning to identify things is an important part of early development. "This is a book". "That is a jar of pickles". "Those are some angry geese". The only reason we can identify these things is because we were taught the right words. If you saw a flock of angry geese without knowing the words "flock of angry geese", you might feel a little stumped (and scared!). Kids need the right words to express not only what they can see, but also how they feel. Knowing words like **puzzled**, **peaceful** and **proud** helps kids identify and express their complex emotions. For example, "I felt **puzzled** when I saw the flock of angry geese start to tap dance".

Developing emotional intelligence is important at any age, but the earlier a child gets in tune with their feelings, the more successful they will be in their personal, social and professional relationships later in life. Vocabulary is a key factor in developing emotional intelligence and we're here to help.

The Book of Big Feelings gives kids the vocabulary they need to express themselves. Research shows that kids who can label emotions like **affectionate**, **aggressive** and **awkward** are more successful in their social interactions and perform better in school.[1] The more words kids have to describe their emotions and the emotions of others, the more nuanced they can be in their approach to the world.

Experts say that kids who can freely express their feelings through language are less likely to act out through tantrums, aggression and defiance. Neuroimaging studies have even shown that communicating emotions helps to calm intense brain activity.[2] In short, having the right words means kids are better equipped to resolve conflict and regulate their responses to emotions.

Encouraging kids to talk about their feelings is part of the journey to developing greater emotional intelligence. Teaching a child about their emotions will help them become mentally resilient, develop coping strategies, make decisions and develop the confidence to handle whatever life throws their way.

1. Pons, F., Lawson, J., Harris, P. L. & de Rosnay, M. (2003). Individual differences in children's emotion understanding: Effects of age and language. *Scandinavian Journal of Psychology*, 44, 347-353.

2. Lieberman, M., Eisenberger, N., Crockett, M., Tom, S., Pfeifer, J. & Way, B. (2007). Putting Feelings into Words: Affect Labelling Disrupts Amygdala Activity in Response to Affective Stimuli. *Psychological Science*, 18(5), 421-428.

On this side, you will find an exploration of the word's meaning. This exploration might be a story, a quiz, a list, an activity, reflection questions, a combination of all of these or none of these at all. Oh, and (most importantly) hilarious illustrations.

Our planet is full of weird and wonderful underwater creatures.

Have you ever seen...

a hairy frogfish?

a vampire squid?

an axolotl?

a yeti crab?

a weedy seadragon?

a giant isopod?

a nudibranch?

an emperor dumbo?

a mola mola?

a guineafowl puffer?

a blobfish?

Aren't you curious to find out more about them?

Oz was feeling cheeky.

She knew she shouldn't draw on Brick's face, but it was too tempting.

She couldn't help herself.

"Gorgeous!" she whispered, with a cheeky giggle.

Luckily, when Brick woke up, he quite liked his new look.

How would you feel if you were Brick?

This is your book, so use it however you want to! Start in the middle, start at the end or you could even start at the beginning if you're feeling traditional. Use it as a word-a-day to kick-start important conversations and help your kids develop their emotional intelligence. Or use it as a dictionary to help your kids identify the emotions they're feeling in that moment.

Use it at the breakfast table. Use it before bed. Use it on the bus.
Use it as a coaster if you really want to (but we'd probably rather you didn't).

HOW TO USE IT

This book is designed for use at home and in the classroom.
Every day, turn the page and discover a new social-emotional word.

On this side, you will find the main word and a big illustration, as well as a definition and word number. The word number will be useful if you ever want to look up a word in the handy glossary at the back of this book.

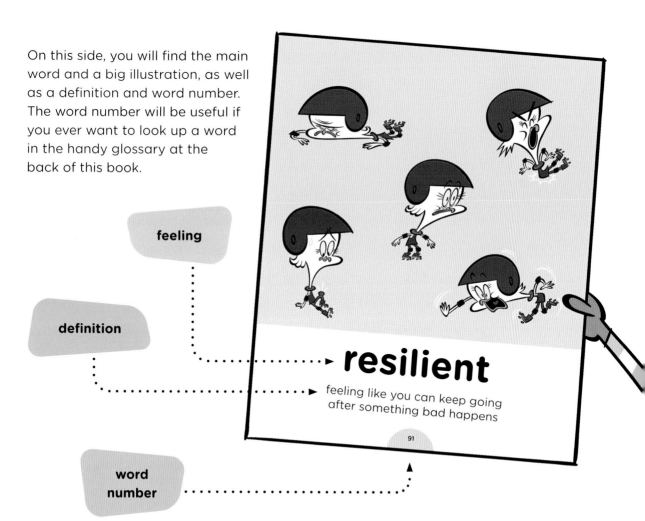

feeling

definition

resilient

feeling like you can keep going after something bad happens

91

word number

Flip this book around to explore each word in further detail...

Having the words to describe your ideal ice cream means you can be sure you'll get given the right flavour.

Having the words to express how you feel helps you and others understand exactly what you're going through.

What ice cream do you feel like today?

FLAVOURS OF FEELING

There are thousands of possible ice cream flavours. You have some basic ones like **vanilla**, **strawberry** and **chocolate**, but why stop there?

As well as **chocolate** ice cream, you can have **chocolate** fudge brownie, mint **chocolate** chip or **chocolate** salted caramel.

Even though all of these are chocolate, they each have their own unique flavour. Chocolate fudge brownie is rich and gooey, mint chocolate chip is cool and refreshing, and chocolate salted caramel is salty and sweet.

Feelings work in the same way. You have some basic ones like **happy**, **sad** and **angry**, but why stop there?

As well as **angry** (11), you can feel **grumpy** (23), **frustrated** (22) or **provoked** (7). Even though these are all angry words, they each have their own unique flavour. **Grumpy** means being in a bad mood, **frustrated** means feeling annoyed that you can't do something, and **provoked** is how you feel when someone is trying to make you angry on purpose.

angry words

for when somebody
has said something mean
to your best friend

annoyed	37
aggressive	47
angry	11
fuming	64
cross	33
frustrated	22
grumpy	23
provoked	7

mindful words

for when you're daydreaming
under a tree on a sunny afternoon

calm	24
relaxed	14
thoughtful	30
pensive	98
reflective	26
quiet	77
peaceful	93

inspiration words

for when you're perfecting
a magnificent finger painting

imaginative	20	passionate	45
inspired	79	focused	21
curious	19		

JUST IN CASE...

Use these shortcuts when you need
to get to a feeling fast!

happy words
for when you've just received
a puppy for your birthday

happy	1
cheerful	28
blissful	35
thrilled	68
elated	118
euphoric	97
uplifted	111

sad words
for when you've lost your
favourite stuffed animal

sad	2
miserable	40
heartbroken	110
disappointed	81
sulky	88
distressed	96

friendship words
for when you've got a playdate
in half an hour

included	53	playful	48
kind	15	shy	71
compassionate	92	sympathetic	32
sociable	72	respectful	117

Sometimes, it's the little things
in life that make us feel happy

...Like Brick and Grit spending the afternoon
splashing around in a swimming pool.

Food makes
Plato feel happy.

Fashion makes
Oz feel happy.

Supporting a friend
makes Bearnice
feel happy.

What makes you feel happy?

happy

feeling full of joy

Sadness is something that we all experience at some point, like when Yin accidentally let go of her balloon.

Sadness shows itself through our bodies, not just our feelings. It can make us cry, or it can make us sleepy or it can make us lose our appetites.

It's okay to feel sad, and it's also okay to ask someone for help when you have trouble cheering yourself up.

sad

feeling unhappy

Everybody feels loved
in different ways.

Armie feels loved
when someone
brings him a hot
chocolate while
he's reading.

Stax feels loved
when someone
recommends
him a song they
think he'll like.

Plato feels loved
when someone
cooks a delicious
meal for him.

Bogart feels loved
when Bearnice hugs him,
but also a little squashed.

What makes you feel loved?

loved

feeling deeply cared for
and appreciated

Grit might have got a bit overexcited
when he saw the bone on TV.

What's the difference between
being excited and being overexcited?

Is there such a thing as too much excitement?

excited

feeling a lot of enthusiasm
and energy

Armie's cure for feeling nervous

(when speaking in front of a crowd)

1 Imagine the audience are all goats.

2 Imagine that the goats are sat on cacti.

3 Imagine that the goats have different moustaches.

4 Imagine that the goats are wearing tutus.

5 Imagine that the goats are juggling watermelons.

Before you know it, you'll be so distracted thinking about moustachioed, tutu-wearing, watermelon-juggling goats that you'll have forgotten all about feeling nervous!

nervous

feeling scared or worried
about something

Bearnice broke her skateboard. She was very upset about it.

Every time she looked at it, she got more and more upset.

She threw her head back and let out a cry.

"I'll never skate again!..." she yelped.

And then on second thought she added, "Probably!"

Why do you think Bearnice is so upset?

What would you say to Bearnice to cheer her up?

Do you think that Bearnice will really never skate again?

upset

feeling sad or worried
about something

Yin was trying to provoke Brick. He wasn't going to let her. He remembered these four simple steps...

1 Stay calm and count to ten.

2 Ask them nicely to stop.

3 Find someone else to play with.

4 If the same person keeps trying to provoke you or others, tell an adult.

At first, Brick had really wanted to break Yin's poking stick in half, but luckily, he followed these wise rules instead.

provoked

when someone makes you
angry on purpose

Yang has unravelled ALL of the toilet roll!
She's also updated Bearnice's shopping list...

Three pints of ~~milk~~ mud

One bunch of ~~bananas~~ beetles

Frozen ~~peas~~ slugs

One punnet of ~~grapes~~ slime

Two bags of mouldy potatoes

~~Tomato~~ goop soup

Two loaves of ~~bread~~ spiders

What is the most mischievous thing you've ever done?

mischievous

feeling like you want to
cause some playful trouble

Bearnice and Plato giggled at jokes all afternoon.

What do porcupines
say after a hug?
Ouch!

What's worse than
finding a worm in your apple?
Finding half a worm in your apple.

What's orange and
sounds like a parrot?
A carrot.

What do you call
a dancing cow?
A milkshake.

What time is it when a lion
walks into the room?
Time to leave!

What do you call a dog
that does magic tricks?
A Labracadabrador.

Can you make up your own joke?

giggly

feeling unable
to stop laughing

Bearnice regretted drawing
all over her favourite dress.

What would you regret the most?

- Ruining your favourite dress
- Forgetting your packed lunch
- Jumping in a muddy puddle while wearing all white
- Getting stuck up a tree
- Eating a mouldy doughnut
- Getting a bad haircut (like Stax!)

regretful

feeling sorry about
something that happened

Oz was angry. Really, really angry.

It's okay to feel angry sometimes, but the way you express it matters. It's important that you don't do something that will hurt yourself or others. Try these healthy ways to manage and express anger.

- Stop and breathe.
- Talk about it with someone you trust, starting with "I feel...".
- Say to yourself, "I can handle this and I will stay in control".
- Imagine a calm, peaceful place.

Don't worry if these tips don't help! Being angry can be a sign of other feelings, like hunger. It might be time for a snack!

angry

feeling very annoyed
and upset about something

"It isn't fair! I deserved to come first!" Yin pouted jealously. She felt sad and angry and worried all at the same time. It was horrible.

Then Bearnice came bounding over.

"Well done, Yin!" said Bearnice. "You were incredible! You came second!"

Yin looked at her prize. Suddenly, a huge grin spread across her face. She felt so proud she thought she might burst. She even felt proud of her sister for coming first.

"Tiger twins rule!!!!" she yelled as she jumped into the air.

Can you remember a time when you felt jealous?

How did you overcome your jealous feelings?

jealous

feeling like you want something
that someone else has

Most of the time,
splitting things
evenly is fair.

Half a cookie
is plenty for Bogart,
who is very small.

But half a cookie
is a very small
portion for Brick
because Brick is big.

Being fair is great. Being generous is even better.
Generous means sharing more than you have to.

What can you do to be generous today?

fair

when something feels
right and equal

Bearnice finds it easy to relax
under a tree on a sunny afternoon.

But sometimes, it can feel impossible to relax when
there are too many things to do and think about!

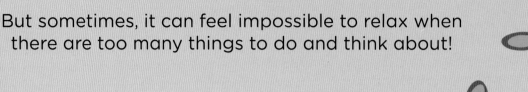

Relaxation tips

- Listen to some gentle music.
- Take a walk outside.
- Doodle.
- Enjoy a cup of hot chocolate.
- Focus on each body part while you stretch it.

How do you like to relax?

relaxed

feeling free
from worries

Being kind means doing caring things for others, like helping your giraffe friend reach his lunch.

Kind things you can do for your friends...

- Make them a delicious sandwich.

- Help them up when they fall down.

- Share your favourite toy with them.

- Help them tidy up, even when you didn't help make the mess.

kind

being friendly
and helpful to others

How will we ever figure out who ate all the cake?

How do you think the other characters feel about Oz eating all the cake?

Do you think Oz feels sorry for being selfish?

Do you think Oz should feel sorry for being selfish?

selfish

only caring
about yourself

Grit didn't realise that his painting
would make Stax feel bad.

"I'm sorry, Stax," said Grit. "I tried my best."

"That's okay, buddy," replied Stax.
"I know you didn't mean to hurt my feelings."

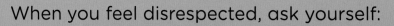

When you feel disrespected, ask yourself:

Did they try to offend me on purpose?

Yes: They were being disrespectful
and you should tell a trusted adult.

No: It was probably a misunderstanding. Explain to
them what upset you and what they should do differently.

disrespected

feeling insulted
or offended

"Oh no," frowned Armie, "how did my vase break?"

Bearnice gulped.

A million excuses ran through her mind...
A sudden earthquake pushed it off the shelf?
A wish-granting genie had been trapped inside the
vase for years and finally broke free? Bogart did it?

After a moment of silence,
Bearnice finally admitted, "It was me. I'm sorry."

"Thank you for being honest," replied Armie.

Why do you think Bearnice chose to be honest?

honest

being truthful
and not telling lies

Our planet is full of weird and wonderful underwater creatures.

Have you ever seen...

a
hairy
frogfish?

a
vampire
squid?

an axolotl?

a
yeti
crab?

a weedy
seadragon?

a
nudibranch?

a
giant
isopod?

an
emperor
dumbo?

a
mola
mola?

a
guineafowl
puffer?

a blobfish?

Aren't you curious to find out more about them?

curious

feeling like you really want
to find out more

All it takes to spark your imagination
is a few questions. **Imagine an alien...**

How many
toes does
it have?

What is its
favourite snack?

How many
eyes does
it have?

What colour is it?

What does it
sound Like?

Does it
have fur?
Or scales?
Or feathers?

Can you
understand what
it's saying?

Does it come in peace
or is it here to take over
the planet?

Woah! You sure do know a lot about this alien.

Why not use all that creativity to draw
a picture or write a story about them?

imaginative

feeling creative
or full of new ideas

Plato was very focused during the spelling test.

Focusing can help you complete a test, read a difficult book or compete in a staring competition like Yin and Yang.

Focusing tips

- Turn off all phones and tablets.

- Turn off the TV.

- Have a glass of water at the ready.

- Sit in a comfortable position.

- Don't blink (only relevant for a staring competition).

focused

feeling like you can really
concentrate on one thing

Oz feels frustrated because her house of cards keeps collapsing.

You can feel frustrated by things happening around you, like a sudden gust of wind blowing down your house of cards.

You can also feel frustrated by things happening inside you, like an emotion you don't understand.

This frustration can make you act out, like Armie, who sometimes snaps his pencils.

Take a break. Everything will feel easier when you're calm. And you'll save a lot of pencils.

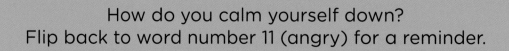

How do you calm yourself down?
Flip back to word number 11 (angry) for a reminder.

frustrated

feeling so annoyed that you can't stand it anymore

grumpy

feeling stuck
in a bad mood

1 Fill a glass with water.

2 Put the glass on a table.

3 Bang on the table with your hands.

Did the water move?
How long did it take for the water to go still again?

No matter how much the water is disturbed, it can always go back to being calm and still. It just takes time.

No matter how angry or upset you get,
you can always go back to being calm too.

calm

feeling still
and relaxed

Armie desperately needs to get to the potty!

Use your finger to trace Armie's path to sweet relief.

relieved

no longer feeling
stressed or worried

Grit had a lot he needed to reflect on.

He found a quiet spot and thought deeply
about his life. Had he been a good dog?

He reflected on the good times.
He reflected on the bad times.

He thought about the times
he had chased his own tail.

He smiled.

Why do you think Grit sat by himself to reflect?

Where is your favourite quiet place to sit and reflect?

reflective

being thoughtful about things
that have happened

You can be as adventurous as
Yin and Yang, wherever you live!

Get out there and explore your local area.

If you're up for a challenge, try to find...

the best view

the biggest Living thing

something surprising

the worst view

the smallest Living thing

"This way, Brick,"
said Grit.

adventurous

feeling like you want to try
new and exciting things

27

Yin and Yang felt cheerful. Today was their birthday picnic and nothing could get them down, no matter what happened.

When their friends were late, they had time to choreograph a brilliant dance routine.

When it started to rain, they spent the afternoon splashing joyfully in muddy puddles.

When they missed the last bus home, they took the opportunity to stop and smell the flowers.

"What an excellent day!" cheered Yin and Yang.

Why do you think Yin and Yang were in such a good mood?

When was the last time you felt cheerful?

cheerful

feeling full of happiness
and smiles

How to put on a hoodie:

- Choose a hoodie to wear.

- Make sure it's the right way round.

- Put your arms through the arm holes.

- Take your arms back out of the arm holes.

- Put one leg through the left arm hole.

- Hop on the other leg ten times.

- Sing "Happy Birthday" backwards.

- Pour milk all over the hoodie.

Grit's directions and Stax's
instructions are both very confusing!

It's always okay to ask questions when you feel confused,
especially when the instructions don't make any sense.

confused

feeling like nothing
makes sense

Stax was very tall.
He was also very thoughtful.

It was raining hard and Stax noticed
that Plato didn't have an umbrella.

He stretched out his long neck
and used his big giraffe head
to protect Plato from the rain.

"Thanks," said Plato.
"That's so thoughtful
of you!"

"I'm your umbrella!" Laughed Stax.

What is the most thoughtful thing
anyone has ever done for you?

What is the most thoughtful thing
you have done for somebody else?

thoughtful

being considerate and taking
the time to think about others

Most people didn't know it,
but Grit was a sensitive puppy.

He didn't act sensitive in most
situations. If anything, he acted
kind of mean and tough.

But he cared about things
— and sometimes he cared a lot.

He especially loved his flower.

When it snapped off
and landed at his feet,
Grit's sensitive
heart broke.

He never
forgot his little
leafy friend.

sensitive

feeling things
very deeply

When Armie's glasses broke,
Brick was very sympathetic.

He felt bad when any
of his friends were upset.

He put his hand on Armie's shoulder
to comfort him and show him
that everything would
be okay.

Armie needed new
glasses, but at least he
had a sympathetic friend.

It can be difficult to know how to help when
someone feels sad. When you want to show
you're feeling sympathetic, try saying:

"I'm here
for you."

"I'm sorry that
happened to you."

"Would you
like a hug?"

sympathetic

understanding how somebody
feels and comforting them

32

cross

feeling annoyed
and showing it

Silliness at its very silliest is about doing things for absolutely no reason at all.

Ways to embrace your inner silliness...

- Speak in a made-up language.
- Pretend to be having an argument with a llama.
- Stick your tongue out.
- Play an imaginary guitar with your nose.
- Wear your socks on your hands.
- Say "six sticky skeletons" five times in a row.
- List made-up facts about snakes.
- Pretend to be a firework.
- **THE FLOOR IS LAVA!**

silly

being ridiculous
or playful

Bearnice was in a blissful mood.

She felt so blissful that she couldn't stop smiling.
She had never been happier!

She sighed merrily and lay back on the grass.

What's making you smile, Bearnice?

What makes you feel blissful?

blissful

feeling completely happy
in every way

Oz stands out from the crowd. Oz is always herself.

Oz wears pink when everyone else wears black.

Oz is prepared when no one else is.

Oz doesn't go to the beach. Oz becomes the beach.

Always be yourself! What makes you different?

different

not being the same
as the others

Armie was starting to get annoyed.

"I'm not in the mood, Brick!" said Armie.

Brick copied him in a silly voice.
"I'm not in the mood, Brick!"

Now Armie really wasn't
in the mood.

Sometimes people try to annoy you on purpose
and sometimes they do it by accident.

Do you think Brick was annoying Armie on purpose?

annoyed

feeling a little
bit angry

37

"No, that glass is half empty," said Grit.

"That glass is half full," said Oz.

"Mmmm," said Yang, mid-gulp.

Each character is viewing this glass of water differently.

Oz is taking an optimistic view, thinking of it as half full.

Grit is taking a pessimistic view, thinking of it as half empty.

Yang, it seems, is just thirsty.

How would you describe the glass of water?

Do you think your answer would be the same every day?

optimistic

feeling positive,
like good things will happen

Armie felt a little muddled.

He wasn't sure exactly what was wrong.

He felt like everything was in the wrong place.

He tried to scratch his head, but he couldn't find his arm.

Even his words were muddled!

"Muddled very feel I," he said.

Get out five items of clothing and put them on the wrong parts of your body! How does that make you feel?

muddled

feeling confused
or jumbled up

Yin and Yang did not want to have a bath.

They didn't want to get wet, splashed, soaked, submerged or, worst of all, bathed.

So, as they sat there on that glum Sunday afternoon, feeling the water seep into their fur, they felt truly miserable.

Sometimes you have to do things you don't want to do, like have a bath.

How do you cheer yourself up when you feel miserable?

miserable

feeling very unhappy
or uncomfortable

Oz was polite.
"After you, Armie."

"Good morning, Oz!
Please and thank you.
Ever so sorry. Goodbye!"
he said, brushing roughly
past Oz without looking at her,
as a book fell off his pile and
landed on her foot with a thud.

She squeaked in pain,
but Armie didn't stop.

You can be polite with words,
but your actions should be polite too.

Armie said several polite things,
but do you think he was actually polite?
What do you think he could do differently next time?

polite

being well behaved
and showing good manners

Some things that aren't rude in your household might be considered very rude in another.

Which of these are considered rude in your house?

Burping Loudly

Talking Loudly

Laughing without covering your mouth

Leaving your shoes on inside the house

Taking the last brownie without asking

Avoiding eye contact

Making a lot of eye contact

Telling someone that you don't like their outfit

rude

showing bad manners

Oz was feeling cheeky.

She knew she shouldn't
draw on Brick's face,
but it was too tempting.

She couldn't help herself.

"Gorgeous!" she whispered,
with a cheeky giggle.

Luckily, when Brick
woke up, he quite liked
his new look.

How would you feel if you were Brick?

cheeky

being a little bit naughty
and playful

We've found two versions of Yang's diary from the day she hurt Grit. In one, she's sorry and in the other, she's not.

Dear Diary,

Today Grit's face got in the way of my baseball. It definitely would have been a home run if he hadn't stopped the ball with his massive head.

Dear Diary,

Today I accidentally hit Grit in the face with a baseball... I feel really bad. I'll have to figure out how to make it up to him.

Which diary entry do you think Grit would prefer and why?

sorry

feeling sad and regretful
about what you did

Being passionate about something
is stronger than just liking it.

You can be passionate about art, music,
science, movies, games, emperor penguin facts,
pasta shapes and so much more...

Armie is passionate about inventing things.

Oz is passionate about art (and herself!).

Plato is passionate about dancing.

What do you feel passionate about?

Ask three people in your life what they're passionate
about and see if anyone has the same passion as you.

passionate

feeling a strong love
or enthusiasm for something

Do you think Brick
regrets being mean?

Do you think Armie
should forgive Brick?

 Dear Armie,

I am so sorry. You have every right to be upset with me and I completely understand if you don't want to talk to me right now.

I shouldn't have stepped on your ear. I was having a bad day and I took it out on you. That was mean.

I hope you can forgive me. Please let me know if there is anything I can do to make you feel better.

From your sorry friend,
Brick

mean

being unkind or unfair
to other people

Sometimes, when Plato felt aggressive, he broke stuff.

When Grit told him his drawing wasn't very good, he snapped his pencils in two. He felt terrible afterwards.

When he found out that Bogart had been using his favourite mug, he smashed it on the floor aggressively. Then he felt even worse.

You're not helping, Plato!

Sometimes, when things go wrong, we can start to feel aggressive. This usually makes the situation worse. Before you act out, head outside to get some fresh air!

aggressive

feeling full of anger
and ready to attack

Feeling playful?
Then it's time to have some fun.

The One-Eyed
Blink

I Want To
Go Home

Face
Scramble

Scaredy Cat

The One-Eyed
Blink 2

Huh?

Tears of Joy

Toothy Grin

Stare Glare

Can you pull these faces?

playful

wanting to goof around
and be silly

Being scared doesn't make you a scaredy cat – everyone feels scared sometimes.

Sometimes people feel scared when they are in dangerous situations, but other times people feel scared by things that others wouldn't find scary at all.

acrophobia
(fear of heights, Like Oz!)

arachibutyrophobia
(fear of peanut butter sticking to the roof of the mouth)

chorophobia
(fear of dancing)

alliumphobia
(fear of garlic)

siderophobia
(fear of stars)

alektorophobia
(fear of chickens)

What helps you when you're feeling scared?

scared

feeling frightened
or afraid

Fight or Flight?

When you feel threatened, you can either stand
up for yourself and others or run away to safety.
Which would you do in these threatening situations?

A family
of hungry
lions move
in next door.

You hear spooky
noises coming from
the garden shed.

Someone
pushes your
friend over.

You poke a pile of leaves
and hundreds of little
spiders come pouring out.

Aliens land in your
garden and demand you
give them all your shoes.

Someone is
teasing you in
the playground.

threatened

feeling scared or intimidated
by something

Plato gave Bearnice
a very sincere apology.

It was obvious that he was
truly very sorry.

"I'm truly very sorry,"
he said in a sincere voice,
with a sincere face.

"I forgive you,"
said Bearnice.
"What did you do?"

Someone who is sincere really means what they say.

How can you tell that someone is being sincere?

sincere

showing your
true feelings

Have you ever heard the expression,
Put yourself in someone else's shoes?

Brick is very empathetic. He can imagine
what it feels like to be anyone and anything.
He can even put himself in a spider's eight
little shoes.

**Different ways to
show someone
empathy:**

Listen and try to
understand their
situation.

If you know them well,
give them a hug or
hold their hand.

Ask what you
can do to help.

empathetic

feeling someone else's pain
or emotions as your own

"Plato, I think we should invite Grit
to join our movie night!" whispered Bearnice.

They had never had a dog at their movie night
before. Previously, it had been a strictly bear
and platypus affair.

"Excellent id-" but before Plato could finish,
Bearnice had scooted across the couch
to make some space.

"Always room for one more!" said Bearnice,
patting the spot next to her.

How do you think Grit felt at the end of the story?

How can you make sure that people feel included?

included

feeling accepted
and part of a group

"Grit and Bogart said I was too tall to ride the roller coaster with them," sniffed Stax.

Bearnice frowned, "Well, it sounds like they wouldn't have been very fun to hang out with."

Stax shrugged, looking down to hide his tears.

"Anyway," she smiled kindly, "I think you're the perfect height to go on the water slide with me!"

Do you think Grit and Bogart excluded Stax on purpose?

How do you think Stax felt when Bearnice included him?

excluded

feeling left out

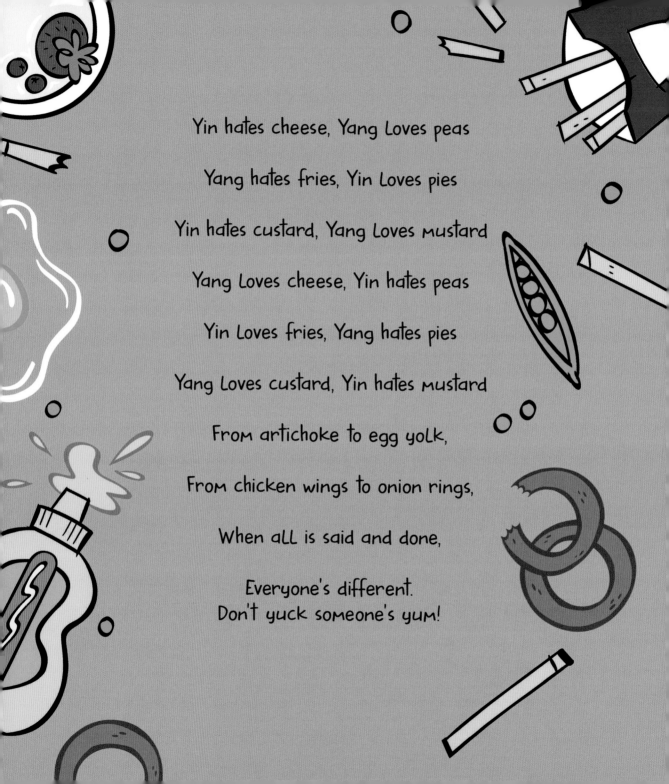

Yin hates cheese, Yang Loves peas

Yang hates fries, Yin Loves pies

Yin hates custard, Yang Loves mustard

Yang Loves cheese, Yin hates peas

Yin Loves fries, Yang hates pies

Yang Loves custard, Yin hates mustard

From artichoke to egg yolk,

From chicken wings to onion rings,

When all is said and done,

Everyone's different.
Don't yuck someone's yum!

disgusted

when you think something
is really gross

Happy birthday, Yin and Yang!

Which of these gifts would you be the most surprised by?

surprised

feeling shocked by something
you didn't expect

Everyone feels worried sometimes.
It might give you a stomach ache or sweaty
hands or make it difficult to concentrate.

When you feel worried:

When you're feeling calmer,
try to challenge your negative thoughts:

Why are you
worrying?

Is it really
a problem?

Is there
a solution?

worried

feeling afraid that something
will go wrong

Stax likes to feel safe.
He feels safe when he rides
his skateboard in a helmet
and knee pads, just like he feels
safe when he holds the hoof
of a trusted grown-up.

What can you do to make yourself feel safe?

**Sing a song
to yourself.**

**Tell yourself that
things will be okay.**

**Give a teddy
a cuddle.**

Most importantly, if you don't feel safe,
you should always tell an adult.

safe

feeling free from
all harm or danger

Brick was
enthusiastic.

"You can do it, Plato!
Just one more level!"
he cheered.

"I haven't even
turned the game
on yet," said Plato.

"You can do it," replied Brick,
just as enthusiastic as before.
"Press the 'on' button!
I believe in you!"

What's something you're enthusiastic about?

enthusiastic

feeling very excited
to do something

Everybody needs to say **I'm sorry** every now and then,
but Brick feels the need to say it twelve times.
In twelve different languages.

samahani
Swahili

أنا آسِف
Arabic

paumanhin
Tagalog

mi dispiace
Italian

прости меня
Russian

undskyld
Danish

lo siento
Spanish

ごめんなさい
Japanese

je suis désolé
French

συγγνώμη
Greek

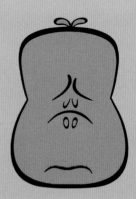

rwy'n flin
Welsh

sinto muito
Brazilian Portuguese

Which of these languages use a different alphabet to English?

Do you know anybody who speaks any of these languages?

apologetic

feeling very, very sorry
about what you did

"Stop!"

cried Bearnice
as she spotted Yang
eating her secret
stash of cookies.

"I'm sorry,"
said Yang with
a nervous smile.

Bearnice didn't
believe Yang, but she
forgave her anyway.
It felt good.

Why do you think Bearnice felt
so good after forgiving Yang?

forgiving

being able to
let go of anger

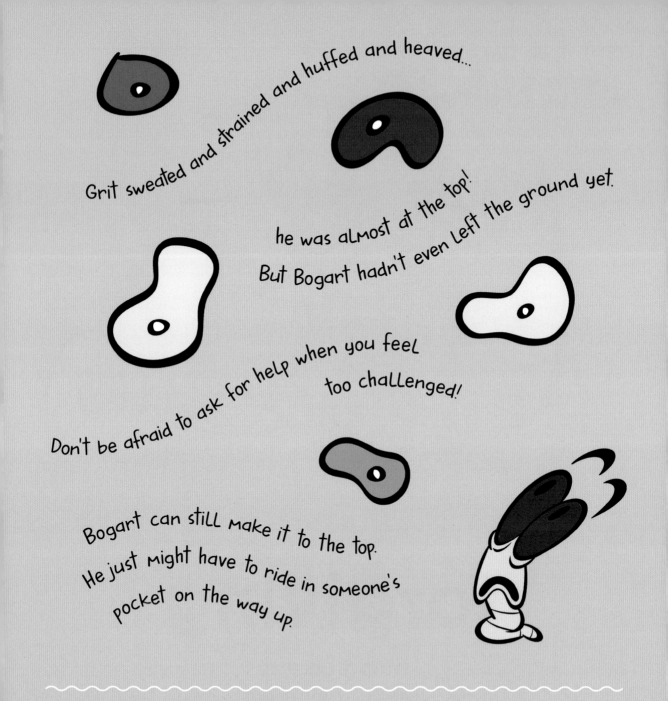

Grit sweated and strained and huffed and heaved...

he was almost at the top!
But Bogart hadn't even left the ground yet.

Don't be afraid to ask for help when you feel too challenged!

Bogart can still make it to the top.
He just might have to ride in someone's pocket on the way up.

What has challenged you the most this week?

challenged

feeling like you're doing
something very difficult

Stax was very, very tired.
He'd been on his feet all day.

Take a break, Stax. Pour yourself
a glass of orange juice!

tired

feeling like you haven't
got any energy left

There are plenty of angry words
and expressions that relate to heat or fire.

My blood is boiling!

Steam is coming out of my ears!

I'm in a burning rage!

I'm feeling hot-tempered!

Why do you think anger is so often related to heat or fire?

What does it feel like to be fuming?

fuming

feeling lots of anger
building up inside

Brick was feeling easygoing. When Yang fell asleep on him, he didn't mind one bit (even though she smelled a bit weird, snored loudly and occasionally dug her claws into his back).

Brick just smiled and kept reading.

easygoing

feeling relaxed and not
easily annoyed

Brick was unique.

He was as unique as a precious flower.

Nobody else was quite like him.

And nobody else is quite like you!

What makes you unique?

unique

being the only one
of its kind

Being bold can mean different
things to different people.

Being bold means
always being yourself,
no matter what.

Being bold means
doing something
other people don't
think you can do.

Being bold means
taking risks.

What kind of bold are you?

bold

feeling ready to take risks
or do risky things

Armie had had so many failed rocket launches.
Sometimes the rocket wouldn't turn on, or a piece
would fall off, or it would just let out a whimper
before falling over.

But one day,
the rocket rumbled.
Then, it roared.
With clouds of smoke
and fire, it FINALLY
lifted off!

Armie jumped up and down,
shouting and waving his arms.
He was so thrilled he thought
he might take off too!

thrilled

feeling very happy
and excited

Feeling tense can be both physical and emotional. Physically, feeling tense is when your muscles are stretched tight or rigid. Emotionally, feeling tense is when you are worried or nervous (and sometimes a little excited too).

Brick's muscles feel tense when he does push-ups.

Armie feels tense waiting for his rocket to launch into space.

Bogart feels tense watching Armie play a video game.

Tense all the muscles in your body.
How does that make you feel?

Now release all that tension and relax.
How does that make you feel?

tense

feeling unable
to relax

While chasing his tail, Grit was horrified to hear a sudden "RRRRIP!"

His trousers had split! His heart-patterned underpants were being shown to the world!

He dashed behind a tree, sure that everybody was pointing and laughing at him. But as he peeked out from behind the branches, he realised that no one was even looking his way.

Remember, the only one focused on your embarrassment is you. Everyone else is too busy thinking about themselves!

What was your most embarrassing moment?

embarrassed

feeling ashamed
and shy

Don't worry Brick,
we don't bite!

shy

feeling nervous
around other people

Sometimes you feel sociable and sometimes
you don't. Whichever way you feel today,
here are some things you can do...

Not feeling sociable

Read your
favourite book.

Play a one-player
video game.

Practise juggling.

Put headphones on
and listen to a song.

Feeling sociable

Write a story
with a friend.

Play a multi-player
video game.

Play football.

Start a band and
write a song together.

It's okay not to feel sociable every day.
Sometimes, you just need to spend some time by yourself.

sociable

wanting to spend time
with other people

Some people think that being brave means not feeling afraid, but that's not true. Being brave means feeling afraid of something but doing it anyway, like when Brick jumped into the water to save his friend.

You can be brave about big things (like going on the world's scariest roller coaster) and you can be brave about little things (like trying a new kind of food).

"Woohoooo!"

screamed Stax and Plato.

Have you been brave this week? How?

brave

feeling ready to do something
that scares you

Which of these would make you feel proud?

- Creating a beautiful work of art
- Sticking your tongue out
- Reading a difficult word on your own
- Having a perfectly polished nose (like Plato!)
- Losing your shoes
- Learning how to ride a bicycle
- Making a friend laugh
- Catching a cold

What have you felt proud about this week?

proud

feeling pleased
with yourself

How to grow a plant

1 Plant a seed in the soil.

2 Water it, make sure it has plenty of sunlight and wait patiently.

3 If the conditions are right, your patience might just pay off.

Plants don't grow right away. You have to be patient. Good things come to those who wait!

patient

being able to wait calmly
for something

Use your finger to trace the consequences.

If you don't wait for your pizza to cool down before biting it...

If you don't wait for your painting to dry before touching it...

If you don't wait for the fresh cement to set before walking down your driveway...

...you might burn your tongue.

...you might get stuck in the cement.

...you might smudge your artwork.

impatient

feeling like you just can't wait
for something to happen

Build your own quiet zone!

When you're feeling tired or sad, it can help to take some quiet time for yourself to listen to music or read a book.

A quiet zone can be anywhere, from under your bed to inside an elaborate blanket fort.

quiet

feeling peaceful
and making no noise

Yang was being horrible.

First, she stole Armie's favourite book.
Next, she stole Plato's frying pan.
Finally, she stole Yin's precious
teddy bear.

"She'll never find me,"
said Yang with a smug smile,
hiding behind a corner.

"I can hear you!" squealed Yin.
"Give me my teddy bear back!"

Do you think feeling smug is a good thing or a bad thing?

smug

feeling pleased with yourself...
maybe a little too pleased with yourself

Inspiration can come
from anywhere.

Armie is inspired
by books.

Plato is inspired
by the sky.

When Plato spotted
a beautiful rainbow,
it sparked his
imagination.

"That gives me an idea
for a cake..." he smiled.

Do you remember the last time you felt inspired?
What did it feel like? What did you do with that inspiration?

inspired

feeling full of ideas
and excited to do something

When Armie arrived at the cinema to watch a movie about a dancing duck, he felt relaxed and happy.

When Armie watched the scene where the dancing duck broke her wing, he felt so gripped that he couldn't look away.

When Armie watched the scene where the dancing duck finally danced again, he felt so moved that he started to cry.

Have you ever felt moved by something? What was it? What did it feel like?

moved

being affected by
a strong feeling, like sadness

Have you ever felt really disappointed? Maybe you were given an incredibly ugly jumper for your birthday, or your school trip was cancelled or you picked up the wrong packed lunch.

Even when you feel disappointed, it's important to be considerate of other people's feelings.

Sometimes it helps to look at the bigger picture.
How much will what's happened affect you tomorrow?
Or in a week? Or in a month?

disappointed

feeling like something isn't
as good as you expected

Bearnice is grateful for her new jumper.
She is also grateful for...

friends

adventures

sunny days

alone time

What are you grateful for today?
List three things!

grateful

feeling thankful

Different people are comforted by different things.

Stax is comforted by music.

Bearnice is comforted by relaxing baths.

Armie is comforted by reading.

Grit is comforted by hugs.

What comforts you?

comforted

feeling reassured
and calm

Sometimes it can feel impossible to decide anything!
Stax can't decide what to eat. Help him choose!

Would you rather eat...

cookies or
brownies?

jelly or
ice cream?

chips or
roast potatoes?

peas or
sweetcorn?

Leaves or
grass?

mud or
toenails?

mouldy apples or
rotten pears?

indecisive

finding it difficult
to make a decision

Have you ever seen such puzzling foods before?

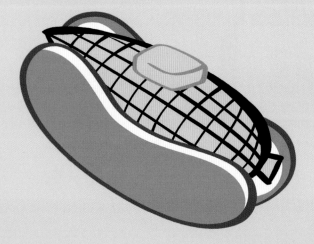

What is so puzzling about them?

Which one do you think would taste the strangest?

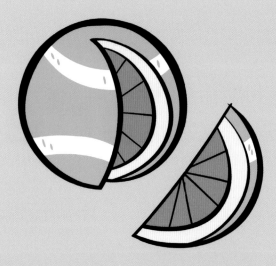

puzzled

feeling confused and unable
to work out what is going on

Oh dear... Realising that there's not even a scrap
of paper left on the roll, Plato has started to PANIC!!

What do you think he should do?

Cry?

Shout for help?

Use his sock?

Wait quietly until
someone accidentally
finds him?

No matter how panicked you are, there's always
a way out... but some ways are better than others.

panicked

feeling very nervous,
worried or scared

Some people say that feeling mortified
is like wishing the ground would
swallow you up.

Why do you think they say that?

Can you think of a time when you felt mortified?

mortified

feeling very
embarrassed

Brick didn't get what he wanted, so he started to sulk.

"Life is so unfair," he thought, staring at his feet.

He sulked down the street and walked straight into a Lamp post.

Brick was stunned for a second. But then he started to giggle.

Why do you think Brick started to giggle at the end of the story, even though he was feeling sulky?

sulky

being quiet and grumpy
and moping about

It feels good to show affection towards the people we love.
It shows them how much we care about them.

Spend some time with them,
Like playing together in the park.

Do something
nice for them,
Like cleaning
their room.

Tell
them
how
much
you
Love
them.

Give
them
a big
hug.

Make a gift for them, Like a sculpture
of their face made out of cheese.

Showing affection can make you feel closer to one another.

affectionate

doing things to show your
love for someone

It's okay to feel a bit timid sometimes, especially when meeting new people.

**Ways to feel comfortable
with new friends...**

Compliment them! Everybody likes to hear something nice.

Practise at home first! Chat with yourself, your family or a pet.

Smile! Smiling invites people to smile back.

You may feel like hiding, but you're probably not the only one who feels timid. Just because somebody seems brave on the outside doesn't mean they feel brave on the inside.

timid

feeling shy
or fearful

Oz rolled out onto the pavement unsteadily, her feet strapped into her gleaming, new roller skates.

No matter how many times she tripped, slipped, stumbled or fell headfirst into a bush... nothing could stop her.

She was resilient.
She was going to make it.

When have you been resilient? How did it feel?

resilient

feeling like you can keep going
after something bad happens

Compassion comes from an old word meaning **sharing in someone's suffering**. When you feel compassionate, you want to help.

Here are some questions you might ask when you're feeling compassionate...

Can I get you a warm drink?

Would you like me to give you a hug?

How can I help?

Do you want to talk about it?

Do you want to go for a walk?

Should we go and do something fun to take your mind off things?

compassionate

feeling somebody else's pain
and wanting to help

How to find peace
(even in the middle of chaos)

1 Sit in a comfortable chair with both feet firmly on the ground. Close your eyes.

2 Take a deep breath, in through your nose and gently out through your mouth. Repeat.

3 Imagine the most magnificent treehouse you've ever seen. Maybe it has big windows or colourful walls. Climb inside. Imagine all the things you love in this treehouse. In this special place, you feel safe and warm.

4 Continue to breathe, in through your nose and gently out through your mouth. Repeat.

5 Take a deep breath and imagine yourself walking down the ladder and out of your treehouse.

6 Slowly and gently, bring your attention back into the room. Wiggle your fingers. Wiggle your toes.

7 Slowly and gently, open your eyes.

peaceful

feeling calm
and quiet

You can feel **physically** exposed, like when you go out on a snowy day wearing only shorts and a T-shirt.

But you can also feel **emotionally** exposed, like when you share your inner thoughts and feelings with others.

You can protect yourself from cold weather by wearing a warm coat and an extra-long scarf.

You can protect yourself from getting your feelings hurt by surrounding yourself with people you trust.

"Brrrr!" shivered Armie.

exposed

feeling vulnerable
and unprotected

Plato is clearly in a very whimsical mood today...
Look at the way he's dressed!

What's the most whimsical outfit you can put together?
Use anything you can find around the house!

whimsical

feeling playful, silly
and imaginative

Oh no! How did you end up there, Stax?

When you're distressed, it can feel like you're dangling dangerously from a height, likely to fall at any moment.

You might feel stuck, but there's always a way down. Sometimes you can ask for help and sometimes you have to do it yourself.

Nicely done, Stax!
But what's that sticking
out of your hoodie?

distressed

feeling extreme worry
or sadness

If you have any of these symptoms,
you might be feeling euphoric!

euphoric

feeling extreme
happiness and joy

There's nothing better than a good, long think.

How would you work out how many hairs are on your head?

What would a cucumber sound like if it could talk?

What's the happiest day you can remember?

If you had a time machine, when and where would you go?

What would a rainbow taste like?

What would someone learn about you if they switched places with you for a week?

pensive

thinking deeply
about things

Help Plato get his fridge organised.

Can you find the objects that don't belong?

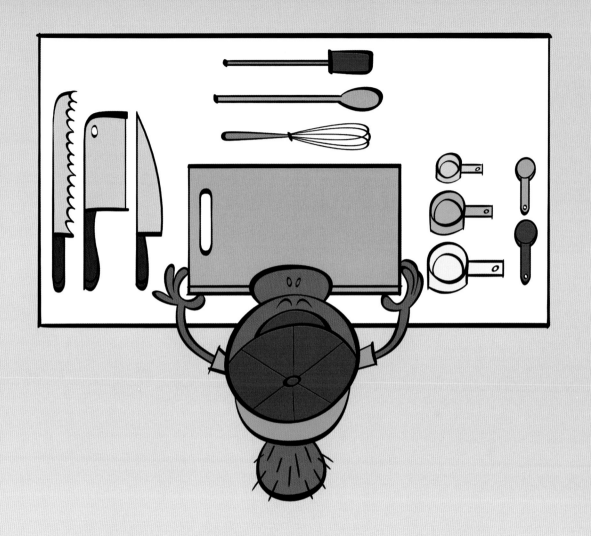

organised

being able to plan carefully
and keep things in order

Oz looked at her incredibly disorganised shoe collection and sighed.

The last time she had tried to tidy it up, she was instantly distracted by a song that came on the radio. After a four-hour sing-along, she was no closer to having tidied up.

This time, she was going to focus on the task at hand.

"I'm not stopping until everything is in its place," she announced.

How do you feel when you walk into a messy room?

How do you feel when you walk into a tidy room?

disorganised

feeling unable to plan carefully
or keep things in order

Brick goes out of his way to help everyone he can.

When Yin and Yang are stuck up a tree,
Brick is the first to fetch a ladder
and help them down.

When Armie needs
help carrying his
shopping, Brick is
the first to volunteer...
even though Armie
lives on the other
side of town.

Why do you think Brick likes to be helpful?

What do you do when someone needs help?

helpful

making things easier
for someone

The twins were amused.
They couldn't stop laughing.

Bearnice, however, was not so amused.

amused

finding something funny

You might feel startled when something unexpected happens, like finding a spider hiding under your tail or a maggot in your burger.

startled

feeling sudden shock
or alarm

sloppy

getting everything,
everywhere

Feeling competitive is a brilliant way to improve at something, but you will never be satisfied if you constantly compare yourself to others.

The best competition is the one you have with yourself.

Choose something you want to improve at, like painting or singing or paper boat making, and see if you can get a little bit better at it every day.

competitive

wanting to win
or be the best

How much is too much?

Stax is juggling comfortably.

Stax is juggling slightly too much.

Stax was juggling far too much.

Trying to do too much at once can be overwhelming.
Stop, take a breath and focus on one thing at a time.

overwhelmed

feeling like there is too much
going on all at once

Being determined means trying hard even when it's difficult or you have a very, very long way to go.

You can do it, Oz!

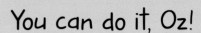

What is something that you are determined to do?

determined

wanting to do something
and not letting anything stop you

"Come on, Let's go," said Brick.
"No," scowled Grit.

"Please?" asked Brick.
"No," scowled Grit again, digging his heels
firmly into the ground.

"Fine, don't have a bath, but you're really
starting to smell," grimaced Brick.

~~~~~~~~~~~~~~~~~~~~~~~~~~~~~~~~~~~~~

How do you think Brick feels about Grit's stubbornness?

Do you think Grit was right to be stubborn?

stubborn

refusing to do something
or change your mind

108

As Grit prepared to jump, he reached out to grab Brick's hand. He knew he could trust him.

When Grit had fallen off his bike, Brick had been there with a plaster.

When Grit needed a friend, Brick was always there for him.

It's important to have people you trust in your life to keep you safe. Remember, if something serious happens, it's always best to talk to a trusted adult.

Why do you think Grit trusted Brick?

trusting

believing that others will do the
right thing and be there for you

Heartbroken means being so sad that
you feel like your heart has broken in half.

Ways to say very sad...

Down in the dumps

Lump in your throat

Feeling blue

Down in the mouth

Reduced to tears

Feeling deflated

heartbroken

feeling very upset
and sad about something

When you feel uplifted, it can feel like you're flying so high that you could touch the stars!

Bearnice is being uplifted by her friends both physically and emotionally.

Physically, they are lifting her up into the air, supporting her with their arms.

Emotionally, they are lifting her mood and emotions, supporting her with their words of encouragement.

When did you last feel like you were flying?

Maybe it was while jumping on a trampoline or after a friend complimented your drawing?

uplifted

feeling full
of happiness

awkward

feeling a little embarrassed
or unsure of what to say

Dodgeball is a brutal sport.
Two teams throwing balls at
each other as hard as they can...
and when you get hit, you're out.

Oz gulped.
She was outnumbered.

As the other team prepared
to attack, Oz backed up against
a wall.

She'd never felt more vulnerable.

Feeling vulnerable isn't always physical – it can be emotional
too. Being emotionally vulnerable could mean talking about
your feelings or revealing something new about yourself.

Can you name someone you trust
enough to be vulnerable with?

vulnerable

feeling like you could
be hurt easily

113

Brick feels most comfortable with himself when he's leaping gracefully through the air, dancing with a red ribbon.

Feeling comfortable is all about feeling relaxed and at ease.

You can feel comfortable in a physical sense, like Bearnice sinking into her favourite armchair.

But you can also feel comfortable in yourself, like accepting yourself exactly as you are.

When do you feel most comfortable with yourself?

comfortable

feeling relaxed and happy
in your own skin

Plato was feeling very guilty after spraying mustard all over Oz.

"Is Oz angry with me? Will she ever forgive me? Will she still want to come to my birthday party next week?"

He couldn't stop thinking about it. He replayed it over and over again in his head.

Don't worry, Plato! It was an accident!

guilty

feeling bad about
something that you did

To Do:

Choose a party outfit.

Remind everyone about Bearnice's party by writing "PARTY TIME!" on the side of a hot-air balloon.

Bake a chocolate cake for Bearnice's party.

Build the world's tallest ice cream sundae for Bearnice's party.

Have a shower.

Fly to Bearnice's party with a supersonic jetpack.

Which of the activities on Stax's to-do list are extravagant?

extravagant

feeling fancy
or over the top

It would have been easy for Bearnice to drop her empty popcorn container on the floor... but then she noticed Plato, who was hard at work tidying the cinema.

Bearnice respected those who worked at her favourite cinema, so she put her empty container in the bin.

What do you do to be considerate and respectful of others and of the environment?

respectful

showing consideration
and respect for others

Different ways to say happy...

- thrilled
- cheerful
- blissful
- euphoric
- uplifted
- elated
- over the moon
- on cloud nine
- on top of the world

When was the last time you felt elated?

elated

feeling so happy
you could almost fly

You might be mesmerised by a pink unicorn like Oz...

...or an unusual flavour combination...

...or an impossible magic trick! Woah, how're you doing that, Yang?

What do you find mesmerising?

mesmerised

feeling like all your attention
is totally held by one thing

Be communicative and tell us about how you're feeling, Bearnice. Let's put your feelings through the Communicator 3000 and see what comes out!

communicative

finding it easy to talk to people
and express yourself

GLOSSARY

A
adventurous, 27
affectionate, 89
aggressive, 47
amused, 102
angry, 11
annoyed, 37
apologetic, 60
awkward, 112

B
blissful, 35
bold, 67
brave, 73

C
calm, 24
challenged, 62
cheeky, 43
cheerful, 28
comfortable, 114
comforted, 83
communicative, 120
compassionate, 92
competitive, 105
confused, 29
cross, 33
curious, 19

D
determined, 107
different, 36
disappointed, 81
disgusted, 55
disorganised, 100
disrespected, 17
distressed, 96

E
easygoing, 65
elated, 118
embarrassed, 70
empathetic, 52
enthusiastic, 59
euphoric, 97
excited, 4
excluded, 54
exposed, 94
extravagant, 116

F
fair, 13
focused, 21
forgiving, 61
frustrated, 22
fuming, 64

G
giggly, 9
grateful, 82
grumpy, 23
guilty, 115

H
happy, 1
heartbroken, 110
helpful, 101
honest, 18

I
imaginative, 20
impatient, 76
included, 53
indecisive, 84
inspired, 79

J
jealous, 12

K
kind, 15

L
loved, 3

M
mean, 46
mesmerised, 119
mischievous, 8
miserable, 40
mortified, 87
moved, 80
muddled, 39

N
nervous, 5

O
optimistic, 38
organised, 99
overwhelmed, 106

P
panicked, 86
passionate, 45
patient, 75
peaceful, 93
pensive, 98
playful, 48
polite, 41
proud, 74
provoked, 7
puzzled, 85

Q
quiet, 77

R
reflective, 26
regretful, 10
relaxed, 14
relieved, 25
resilient, 91
respectful, 117
rude, 42

S
sad, 2
safe, 58
scared, 49
selfish, 16
sensitive, 31
shy, 71
silly, 34
sincere, 51
sloppy, 104
smug, 78
sociable, 72
sorry, 44
startled, 103
stubborn, 108
sulky, 88
surprised, 56
sympathetic, 32

T
tense, 69
thoughtful, 30
threatened, 50
thrilled, 68
timid, 90

tired, 63
trusting, 109

U
unique, 66
uplifted, 111
upset, 6

V
vulnerable, 113

W
whimsical, 95
worried, 57

MADE WITH LOVE BY MRS WORDSMITH'S CREATIVE TEAM

Creative Director

Craig Kellman

Writers

Tatiana Barnes
Justin Blanchard
Katie Davis
Mark Holland
Amelia Mehra
Jill Russo

Pedagogy

Rochelle McClymont
Eleni Savva

Art Directors

Phillip G Mamuyac
Nicolò Mereu
Daniel J Permutt

Lead Designer

James Sales

Academic Advisor

Natascha Crandall

Artists

Brett Coulson
Giovanni D'Alessandro
Aghnia Mardiyah
Maggie Mikan

Designers

Holly Jones
Lady San Pedro
James Webb

Project Managers
Senior Editor Helen Murray
Senior Designer Anna Formanek
Project Editor Lisa Stock

Senior Production Editor Jennifer Murray
Senior Production Controller Lloyd Robertson
Publishing Director Mark Searle

First published in Great Britain in 2023 by
Dorling Kindersley Limited
A Penguin Random House Company
DK, One Embassy Gardens, 8 Viaduct Gardens,
London, SW11 7BW

The authorised representative in the EEA is
Dorling Kindersley Verlag GmbH. Arnulfstr. 124,
80636 Munich, Germany.

10 9 8 7 6 5 4 3
003-329279-Feb/2023

A CIP catalogue record for this book
is available from the British Library.
ISBN 978-0-24156-739-5

Printed and bound in China

For the curious

www.dk.com

mrswordsmith.com

MIX
Paper | Supporting
responsible forestry
FSC™ C018179

This book was made with Forest
Stewardship Council™ certified
paper - one small step in DK's
commitment to a sustainable future.
**For more information go to
www.dk.com/our-green-pledge**

THE END OF THE BOOK
DOESN'T MEAN THE END OF THE FUN!

READICULOUS®

Boost your child's confidence and help them master the five building blocks of literacy – phonemic awareness, phonics, fluency, vocabulary and comprehension – with the learn-to-read adventure game Readiculous!

Made with world-leading experts in literacy and child development

Using a curriculum-aligned framework

Including progress tracking for parents

Featuring pedagogically designed challenges and minigames

Starring characters designed by award-winning, Hollywood artists

Go on an adventure with our outrageous cast of characters and discover their stories!
Available now on iOS and Android.

Ages 4-7

Download on the
App Store

GET IT ON
Google Play

SCAN TO GET THREE MONTHS FREE

The building blocks of reading

READING COMPREHENSION
VOCABULARY
FLUENCY
PHONICS
PHONEMIC AWARENESS

READ TO LEARN

LEARN TO READ

Phonemic Awareness → Phonics → Fluency → Vocabulary → Reading Comprehension

READICULOUS®

Readiculous App
App Store & Google Play

Word Tag App
App Store & Google Play

OUR JOB IS TO INCREASE YOUR CHILD'S READING AGE

This book adheres to the science of reading. Our research-backed learning helps children progress through phonemic awareness, phonics, fluency, vocabulary and reading comprehension.